All Kinds of Feelings

Written by Judith Heneghan

Illustrated by Ayesha Rubio

CRABTREE
PUBLISHING COMPANY
WWW.CRABTREEBOOKS.COM

CRABTREE
PUBLISHING COMPANY
WWW.CRABTREEBOOKS.COM

Author: Judith Heneghan

Editorial director: Kathy Middleton

Editors: Nicola Edwards, Ellen Rodger

Illustrators: Ayesha Rubio, Jenny Palmer

Proofreader: Crystal Sikkens

Designer: Little Red Ant

Prepress technician: Margaret Salter

Print coordinator: Katherine Berti

Library and Archives Canada Cataloguing in Publication

Title: All kinds of feelings / written by Judith Henghan ; illustrated by Ayesha Rubio.
Names: Heneghan, Judith, 1965- author. | Rubio, Ayesha L., illustrator.
Description: Series statement: All kinds of people | Previously published: London: Franklin Watts, 2019. | Includes index.
Identifiers: Canadiana (print) 20190200553 | Canadiana (ebook) 201902005561 | ISBN 9780778768036 (hardcover) | ISBN 9780778768074 (softcover) | ISBN 9781427124241 (HTML)
Subjects: LCSH: Emotions—Juvenile literature.
Classification: LCC BF531 .H46 2020 | DDC j152.4—dc23

Library of Congress Cataloging-in-Publication Data

Names: Heneghan, Judith, 1965- author. | Lopez Rubio, Ayesha, illustrator.
Title: All kinds of feelings / written by Judith Heneghan ; illustrated by Ayesha Rubio.
Description: New York, NY : Crabtree Publishing Company, 2020. | Series: All kinds of people | Includes index.
Identifiers: LCCN 2019043499 (print) | LCCN 2019043500 (ebook) ISBN 9780778768036 (hardcover) | ISBN 9780778768074 (paperback) | ISBN 9781427124241 (ebook)
Subjects: LCSH: Emotions in children--Juvenile literature. | Emotions--Juvenile literature.
Classification: LCC BF723.E6 H46 2020 (print) | LCC BF723.E6 (ebook) | DDC 155.4/124--dc23
LC record available at https://lccn.loc.gov/2019043499
LC ebook record available at https://lccn.loc.gov/2019043500

Crabtree Publishing Company
www.crabtreebooks.com   **1-800-387-7650**
Published by Crabtree Publishing Company in 2020

Published in Canada
Crabtree Publishing
616 Welland Avenue
St. Catharines, ON
L2M 5V6

Published in the United States
Crabtree Publishing
PMB 59051
350 Fifth Ave, 59th Floor
New York, NY 10118

Printed in the U.S.A./012020/CG20191115

First published in Great Britain in 2019 by The Watts Publishing Group
Copyright © The Watts Publishing Group 2019

Contents

Feelings matter.

Things that happen around us affect how we feel inside.

And how we feel inside often shows on the outside.

The way we feel may change many times throughout the day.

It's my birthday and I feel excited!

I feel impatient. When's the party going to start?

Now I feel shy.

Grandpa arrives and makes me feel special!

Thank you!

I'm so happy!

I feel sad when we say goodbye.

Maybe you feel excited.

It's natural to feel **curious** about the world around us.

Questions bubble up inside, bursting to escape.

What is it like to live under a log?

Why do spiders build webs?

We wonder, we daydream.

And sometimes we feel impatient!

Hurry up, butterfly!

Everyone makes mistakes or
has an accident, now and then.

When we feel **embarrassed**, our cheeks may grow hot or change color. It doesn't last very long.

Next time I'll look where I'm going!

Luckily, accidents can help us learn.

Sometimes the world feels like a big, noisy place. You might feel quite small. Everyone else is busy, or talking, or playing, or learning, and you feel as if you are alone.

We all feel lonely sometimes. It's okay. You will find a friend. It might be someone who feels just like you do.

Meeting new people often makes us feel shy.

But when we make new friends, we stop feeling shy. Good friends make us feel happy, confident, and strong.

With my friends I can be myself!

My friends make me feel giggly!

Anger is a big feeling. It's a scary feeling.

When something upsets us, or annoys us, or **frustrates** us, it can feel like there is a firework inside that wants to explode.

I hate math!

Sometimes we shout, hit, or run off. Anger can feel hard to control.

Later, when things are calmer, we may feel sorry.

Sometimes people show their feelings in unexpected ways. Feelings can be confusing!

I laugh when I feel nervous.

I shout when I'm excited.

Sometimes it is difficult to know how someone else is feeling.

Love isn't a **complicated** feeling. It's simple.

Love makes us feel happy and safe.
It makes us feel good about ourselves.

Love can be loud or quiet. It can feel like a warm hug, a deep laugh, or a soft, singing breeze.

Feeling loved helps us love back.

When we talk about our feelings, we help others understand what's really going on inside us.

I loved being the winner.

We start to understand ourselves. We start to understand each other, too.

Feelings are important.

Every feeling is normal.

Your feelings help make you who you are.

Feelings make us feel alive!

How do you think these children are feeling?

Notes for teachers, parents, and caregivers

This book aims to encourage children to talk about their feelings, recognize and value a range of emotions in themselves and those around them, and develop empathy for the way other people may be feeling. The text and images are designed as prompts for discussion, either at home with a parent or caregiver, or in a classroom setting.

Young children can be encouraged to explore, understand, and articulate their own and each other's feelings in a variety of ways. For example, parents and caregivers can ask a child to look at the different feelings shown throughout the book and say if or when they have felt the same. However, the book should be used sensitively in a classroom setting. If a child discloses feelings of sadness or fear associated with their home life, they may need reassurance that they don't have to share this with their peers, but that they can talk to their teacher or another trusted adult instead.

Here are some additional activities that support and expand on the scenarios shown in the book.

How do we show our feelings?

Show children a range of different facial expressions cut from magazines or drawn on flashcards. Ask them how they think that person is feeling. How can they tell? Can they make that face themselves? Discuss how sometimes we express our feelings in different ways, for example, by hiding, shouting, or being quiet. Why do we sometimes try to hide our feelings?

Changing feelings

Children can be helped to understand that feelings can change quickly, just like the weather. Make a "feelings barometer" by cutting out a large circle from a plain piece of cardboard and dividing it into six segments, like slices of pie. Draw a picture of a different type of weather in each segment, for example: sunny, rainbow, raining, thunder and lightning, foggy, chilly, or sunshine and showers.

Attach an arrow to the middle with a paper fastener. In the classroom: ask children to match different feelings to different types of weather, and discuss whether there is a general class atmosphere or mood at any point in the day. At home: encourage your child to turn the arrow to indicate how they are feeling throughout the day.

Creative expression

Music is a wonderful way for young children to explore different feelings. Play a piece of instrumental music that has loud and soft sections, slow and fast sections, and ask them to describe how they feel at different moments in the piece. Alternatively, explore feelings using simple percussion instruments or painting with different colors and brushstrokes.

Coping with strong feelings

Strong feelings can be overwhelming for young children. Teachers, parents, and caregivers can support them by providing a safe way to acknowledge how they feel. Use markers on uninflated balloons of different colors to draw faces that are excited, angry, and nervous, for example. Then fill the balloons with rice, using a funnel, and tie a knot in the opening. Explain that these are the child's balloon buddies. When they have a strong feeling, they can select the balloon that matches how they feel and squeeze it for as long as they need to.

Responding to others

Encourage children to think about how they might respond to each other's feelings. For example: being kind when someone is sad, or sitting next to someone who looks lonely, or telling a teacher if someone is hurt or upset.

Useful words

complicated   Hard to understand or explain

curious   How it feels when you want to find out about something

embarrassed   How it feels when people are looking at you and you don't want them to

frustrated   How it feels when you want to do something but you can't

impatient   How it feels when you want something or someone to hurry up

proud   How it feels when you have achieved something new

Index